Logan Pass

by

JERRY DeSANTO

---

with photography by

MICHAEL S. SAMPLE
and others

FALCON™

Acknowledgments

Clare Landry, Lynne Murdock, and Cindy Nielsen of Glacier National Park helped me get going on this project. John Grassy of Falcon Press kept me on track. Special thanks to Kathy Johnson for accurate word processing on short notice, for the correction of factual errors, and for editorial advice.

———————

Design, typesetting, and other prepress work by Falcon Press, Helena, Montana.
Printed in Korea.

Cataloging-in-Publication Data
DeSanto, Jerry.
　　Logan Pass: a visitor's guide to the Logan Pass area of Glacier National Park/
　　Jerry DeSanto.
　　p. cm.
　　ISBN: 156044-158-5
　　1. Glacier National Park (Mont.) — Guidebooks.　　I. Title.
　　F737.G5D4 1995
　　917.86'52 — dc20　　　　　　'95-9692 CIP

about Glacier National Park

Glacier became a national park with President William Howard Taft's signature on May 11, 1910. Set aside as a unique example of the role of glaciers in molding the landscape, this remarkable place had what American naturalist John Muir called "the best care-killing scenery on the continent" after a visit in the 1890s. Muir marveled at the "beautiful lakes derived straight from glaciers, lofty mountains ... and meadowy gardens abounding in the best of everything."

Glacier's more-than-a-million acres include spectacular mountain vistas, waterfalls hundreds of feet high, and lakes, either crystal-clear or colored by the erosive effects of active glaciers. In the summer, its meadows, prairies, and slopes are mantled with brilliant wildflowers. Everything is surrounded by the dark green of forests threaded by sparkling rivers and streams.

Going-to-the-Sun Road. GLENN VAN NIMWEGEN

about Logan Pass

Logan Pass was named for Major William R. Logan, Glacier's first superintendent from 1910 to 1912. The pass cuts across the Continental Divide at the relatively low elevation of 6,680 feet above sea level. American Indians traveled over Logan Pass periodically during the last 10,000 years. It was also known later as Trapper's Pass, with a long-abandoned trail reaching it from the east side.

Going-to-the-Sun Road, one of America's outstanding scenic roadways,

was completed in 1932 and opened to public use in 1933. Dedication ceremonies on July 15, 1933, drew 5,000 visitors, a crowd even by today's standards. Ever since, Logan Pass has been a primary attraction in Glacier and a visit to this mountain wonderland is an unforgettable experience for millions of people.

In 1929 Park Naturalist George C. Ruhle recommended the name Going-to-the-Sun Road to replace the earlier monikers of Trans-mountain Road and Logan Pass Road. Ruhle was inspired by Going-to-the-Sun Mountain, from Logan Pass the dominant peak on the eastern skyline.

the Setting

One-third of Glacier National Park lies above the tree limit and is classified by ecologists as "subalpine" or "alpine." This mountainous terrain makes it a special place among the national parks, and Logan Pass is a special place within Glacier National Park.

"When we try to pick out anything by itself," John Muir wrote, "we find it hitched to everything else in the universe." Logan Pass is a perfect example of Muir's eloquent statement. The geology, the weather, and the plant and animal life here are spread out in all their diversity—yet everything has a place in the greater picture.

The rocks here are over one billion years old, among the oldest on earth. Thanks to a series of remarkable geologic events, they are visible today on mountain faces, ridges, and slopes. The creation of today's landscape began when layers of rock were deposited in a sea-filled trough. Millions of years passed. Then, approximately 60 to 70 million years ago, a period of mountain building uplifted the thousands of feet of rock. Following this event, a titanic earth movement at a place known as the Lewis Overthrust Fault slowly pushed a mantle of the underlying ancient rock over the younger layers, eventually moving this overriding slab some 40 miles to the

Beargrass near Logan Pass. Ed Cooper

northeast. This "overthrust" took millions of years to unfold, and may still be moving today at far less than a snail's pace.

Erosion then worked to produce the scenery of today. The ice of glaciers, freezing and thawing, wind, and the water of streams have combined to wear down, carve, and mold the mountainscape that is Logan Pass. These processes continue, though at a rate immeasurably slow by mortal standards. Now and then a flood or a landslide speeds up this methodical project. Such spectacular events, while memorable, are only minor episodes in the vast expanse of time.

Though modern visitors see active glaciers and a glacially carved park, it is not these living glaciers that made this region what it is today. Glacier is truly an Ice Age park: its mountainscape is the result of glacial action during the Pleistocene epoch, or Ice Age. During that epoch, lasting from about two million to 10,000 years ago, glaciers overran much of North America. Filling valleys with hundreds of vertical feet of ice and blanketing all but the highest peaks, they covered at least 90 percent of the Glacier Park area. The valleys east and west of Logan Pass were rivers of ice; the meadowy garden of Logan Pass was rock, buried beneath the same ice.

Today's glaciers are not remnants of their much larger cousins; instead, they are the products of a recent cold period that reached its peak about 140 years ago. These modern glaciers are steadily shrinking. Some have disappeared completely in recent years, victims of little snowfall and warmer temperatures. Yet they do the same work as the great Pleistocene glaciers, though on a much smaller scale.

No other place in Glacier has such an open expanse of green, flower-dotted subalpine meadows, treeless alpine flower beds, and snow-fed streams as Logan Pass. There are many reasons for the unique qualities of this area. The openness here is partially explained by the gentle slope of the terrain, allowing the buildup of soils favorable to low-growing plants. Year after year, frost turns and sorts rocks and soil. Favorable niches are created for plants with specific requirements, then altered again by relentless freezing and melting. Change is constant in this dynamic environment.

The alignment of ridges favorable to the growth of trees and of intervening wet glades where trees cannot take root accounts for the "ribbon forest" and tree islands of Logan Pass. The scarcity of trees may be the result of fires of long ago, when the forest here was continuous. Revegetation has been incomplete and traces of the fires have vanished, perhaps swept away by avalanches.

Unexpectedly, the grizzly bear plays an important role at Logan Pass. Bears tear up the soil in many places in their search for underground plant parts and burrowing animals. A current study indicates that grizzly activity could be a major agent in shaping the variety of plant life here, including the relative absence of trees at Logan Pass today.

The long, snowy winter provides most of the moisture required for the brief summer at Logan Pass. Deep mountain snow is nature's own reservoir, and far more efficient than the manmade variety. The insulating blanket of snow also protects plants and determines the seasonal distribution of birds and mammals.

Mountain plants have made many adaptations to cope with the seasonal cycles. Most important is their ability to grow and reproduce in a brief span of time. The presence or absence of trees is also closely controlled by the length of the seasons. Every plant, no matter how hardy, requires a growing season. Trees usually need about two months with no more than a light frost. Some low-growing plants may be able to continue living with a one-month period for growth.

Coping with winter is a simple matter for ground squirrels, marmots, and bears: their response is to hibernate. Some smaller mammals remain in this deepest of sleep for nine months. Mountain goats remain in the high country all year, and depend on wind-blown areas to reach their winter browse. Despite their mountaineering skills, goats are occasionally caught in avalanches. In spring, their remains become a welcome protein boost for bears emerging from hibernation.

A winter visitor to Logan Pass may see a golden eagle soaring high in the sky above the whitened landscape. Mountain goats will be picking their way across ledges, only slightly less white than the unbroken snow. A startling explosion of white could only be a ptarmigan, one of the few active wintertime residents. Camouflaged in white and feathered to its toes, the ptarmigan is well-adapted to the color and temperature of winter.

Humans have played no part in the evolution of the mountainscape at Logan Pass. Their presence cannot enhance what nature has created. The preservation of this fragile mountain ecosystem and the accommodation of millions of visitors is a great challenge for the National Park Service.

What is the
Continental
Divide? *Can I see it from Logan Pass?*

Known as the Backbone of the World to early American Indians, the Continental Divide is the topographical fenceline that separates the major continental drainages. Originating in Alaska's Brooks Range and ending at the Straits of Magellan at the tip of South America, the Continental Divide is at least 25,000 miles long.

In Montana the divide begins at Monument 272 on the 49th parallel in Glacier, ending in Yellowstone National Park 800 miles to the south. The lowest point along the divide in Montana is 5,215 feet at Marias Pass in Glacier. The highest is Eighteenmile Peak at 11,141 feet, in southwest Montana.

From Logan Pass, waters flow westward to the Pacific Ocean and eastward via the Saskatchewan River drainage to Hudson Bay. The visitor center lies a few hundred feet east of the divide; a hiker crosses it three times en route to Hidden Lake Overlook. The location of the divide usually can be clearly recognized in steep, mountainous terrain; it is not so easy to detect in the rolling, forested country of Yellowstone Park.

Triple Divide Peak, about 13 miles southeast of Logan Pass, is unique. From that point 8,020 feet above sea level, water flows in three directions by way of Pacific Creek, Hudson Bay Creek, and Atlantic Creek, eventually reaching the Pacific Ocean, Hudson Bay, and the Atlantic Ocean.

Moonrise over the Continental Divide. George Wuerthner

Grizzly bear tracks. Michael S. Sample

April	April
Grizzly bears emerge from winter dens.	Road crews begin clearing Going-to-the-Sun Road at lower elevations.

Do people climb these mountains?

"Most visitors to the park are so moved by the views from this spectacular pass," wrote J. Gordon Edwards, Glacier's patron saint of climbing, "that they do not consider going any higher." The majority of visitors may stay at Logan Pass, but plenty of them have continued upward: all of the mountains seen from the pass have been climbed many times, and by many different routes.

Any climber who has explored Glacier knows that most of the rock in the park cannot be trusted. Seemingly secure handholds and footholds can disappear instantly, and as a result technical climbing is not popular. Climbing in Glacier, "pleasant, although strenuous" according to Edwards, more often takes the form of exhilarating ridge walks ending in far-ranging summit views.

Steep snowfields are frequently and sometimes fatally attractive to unskilled climbers. In Glacier more accidents have been caused by falls from snowfields than from rocks.

Climbers of these high, remote peaks often have the mountains to themselves. But unexpected meetings sometimes happen. In 1982 a pair of climbers bivouacking on Mount Cleveland met two grizzly bears at the summit of this 10,466-foot peak. All went their separate ways.

All climbers at Logan Pass should register at the visitor center. Not only is this a wise precautionary measure, but much information is available from rangers. Every climber in Glacier should consult *A Climber's Guide to Glacier National Park* by J. Gordon Edwards.

MICHAEL S. SAMPLE

Top right: On the rocks near Logan Pass.
DARRIN SCHREDER

Bottom right: Climbing Reynolds Mountain.
DARRIN SCHREDER

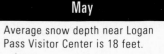

May

Average snow depth near Logan Pass Visitor Center is 18 feet.

Why are the
trees so
stunted?

Subalpine fir is the most abundant tree at Logan Pass. Scattered among the fir thickets is an occasional whitebark pine and rarer still is an Engelmann spruce. Large whitebark pines may be seen along the shores of Hidden Lake, but most of them are dead or dying, victims of disease, pine beetles, and, perhaps, of recent climate changes.

Trees are near their upper elevational limit at Logan Pass. They have adapted to the cold of winter and the severe frosts of spring and fall, but they cannot live with more than a light frost during the short growing season. For trees at Logan Pass, the temperatures of June, July, and August are the most critical of the year. Subalpine fir will grow where temperatures reach 40 degrees below zero in winter—but they will not take root in a site that receives many cold days in summer.

Many of the trees growing in clusters or "islands" around Logan Pass are clones, meaning that all of the trees in an island share one root system and are actually one prolific tree. Clones often appear as a dome-shaped outline, with the oldest "parent" tree in the center. The upright stems of clone trees appear progressively shorter as new growth continues to emerge at the edge of the island.

Wind and snow depth control the

MICHAEL S. SAMPLE

Mid May

Mountain goat kids are born. (Kid pictured at left.)

Tree islands and Reynolds Mountain. Michael S. Sample

shape and height of trees at Logan Pass. Wind is an effective pruning shears, creating the "flagging" effect of branches streaming outward on the downwind side. In winter the deformed upright trunks stand above the snow-covered fir thickets, continually battered by the wind and snow.

What do the animals up here eat?

Under natural conditions animals eat natural food and nothing is provided by humans. Grizzly bears, mountain goats, bighorn sheep, ground squirrels, and marmots get along very well without garbage or handouts. A few unfortunate animals become addicted to human food and find themselves in trouble.

Many Logan Pass animals are vegetarians, grazing and browsing in the high meadows. The brief summer is very important to these animals, which spend the majority of their waking hours eating.

Bears and some ground squirrels are omnivorous—they will eat whatever they can find. Naturalist John Muir observed that, for the grizzly bear, "almost everything is food except granite." Such opportunistic feeding habits ensure that the animal will find something to eat if one food source becomes unavailable. Most animals live in a feast-or-famine cycle. When food is abundant, a grizzly bear, for example, will eat 50 pounds of carrion in one day. During lean times, however, the same bear may go days with little or nothing to eat.

Plants make up the vast majority of the food eaten by animals in the Logan Pass area. Carrion, devoured by bears and ground squirrels, represents a smaller if equally important source of food. Ground squirrels and marmots, in turn, are unearthed and eaten by bears at certain times of the year.

Least chipmunk. MICHAEL S. SAMPLE

Bighorn sheep. Michael S. Sample

Mid May

American pipit, rosy finch, and white-crowned sparrow (pictured) return to Logan Pass.

How much
snow falls here
in the winter? *How cold does it get?*

There is no year-round weather station at Logan Pass. Two nearby stations, however, measure and record precipitation. About 500 inches of snow falls during a typical winter at these stations, and Logan Pass probably receives a similar amount. Some snow melts, some is blown into huge drifts, and the remainder is compacted. December and January are the snowiest months, when about 100 inches collects each month, an average of three inches per day.

A weather station near Grinnell Glacier, about five miles from Logan Pass, recorded an almost-unbelievable 147 inches of precipitation annually over an 11-year period. Compare this total with the annual 23 inches at snowy Polebridge on the west side of Glacier and you can appreciate the severity of mountain weather.

The coldest temperature registered in Glacier is 55 degrees below zero, recorded at 5,215 feet at Marias Pass in January of

1959. Logan Pass may have been even colder that day, since temperature drops an average of three to five degrees for every thousand feet of elevation gained. And Logan Pass may have been as cold as Rogers Pass in Montana, 135 miles southeast, where a reading of 70 degrees below zero was recorded on January 20, 1954—a national record that has yet to be broken.

Near the end of March, when winter snow reaches its greatest depth, Logan Pass is buried beneath about ten feet of snow. Some winters have much more snow, some less. In the mountains of Montana there is no such thing as a "normal" or "average" winter.

A reliable indicator of snow depth is the Big Drift, less than a mile east of Logan Pass. Big Drift is *the* biggest drift along Going-to-the-Sun Road, measuring up to 80 feet deep in some years.

Logan Pass in winter. Michael S. Sample

Who *or what* are the mountains named for?

Reynolds Mountain, the prominent horn peak directly south of the visitor center, was named for Charles B. Reynolds, an editor whose connection to the park was his friendship with explorer George Bird Grinnell. Some people believe the name refers to Albert "Death-on-the-Trail" Reynolds, a legendary ranger of Glacier's early years. Indeed, it seems more appropriate to recognize Death-on-the-Trail than Charles B.

Clements Mountain and Pollock Mountain were named for commissioners who, along with Grinnell, negotiated the sale of Blackfeet Indian lands in 1895. These lands now make up the eastern half of the park. Another early explorer, Dr. Lyman B. Sperry, named Mount Oberlin after Oberlin College in Ohio. Sperry Glacier honors his memory.

Grinnell was an important figure in the Glacier area for 40 years. He is commemorated elsewhere in the park by a glacier, a lake, a mountain, a point, a waterfall, and a geologic formation.

Bearhat Mountain was named for a Kootenai chief, and

Clements Mountain and wild strawberries.
MICHAEL S. SAMPLE

Heavy Runner and Reynolds Mountain. DARRIN SCHREDER

Heavy Runner Peak after a well-known Blackfeet chief. The name of Going-to-the-Sun Mountain probably refers to Napi, the Old Man of the Blackfeet, who descended from the sky to help his children, then rose again via this mountain. Several versions of this story exist, including at least one version preserved in the writings of James Willard Schultz.

Early June

Bighorn sheep lambs are born.

Did American Indians use Logan Pass?

American Indians living west of the mountains crossed Logan Pass traveling to and from the Buffalo Plains. Tribes from the east also used the pass on raiding forays to the west. Since the heavily wooded valleys on both sides of the pass would have made horse travel very difficult, the time of use almost certainly predated the introduction of the horse. This may explain the route's original name—The Ancient Road. The line of travel at that time would have followed Logan Creek and Reynolds Creek, not the path of today's paved road.

According to James Willard Schultz, who lived with the Blackfeet many years, all of the mountains, glaciers, and streams at Logan Pass bear Blackfeet names. Hanging Gardens, the flowery meadow just south of the visitor center, was once known as "Big-Feet Was Killed." Schultz tells a story of Blood Indians killing a caribou there (caribou have very big feet), then naming the place after this event.

The pass also was used by Kootenai, Salish, and Shoshoni people. Each tribal group bestowed its own names upon various features of the area. Recent ar-

Early June

Logan Pass Visitor Center and Going-to-the-Sun-Road usually open.

MICHAEL S. SAMPLE

chaeological findings prove that American Indians have used the high country of Glacier National Park for thousands of years. It is believed that modern Indians used the area extensively until the near-extinction of the buffalo in the late nineteenth century. Going back farther in time, Indian occupation ebbed and flowed with long-term fluctuations in the climate.

Hanging Gardens. Michael S. Sample

What birds *are here in* the summer? In the winter?

White-crowned sparrows are the most noticeable summer birds at Logan Pass. Twittering, hopping through fir thickets, these tiny birds are almost always moving, though they occasionally perch on treetops to sing their whistling songs. Rosy finches and American pipits are true mountaineers, passing the summer at high elevations in Glacier. Flocks of sociable rosy finches busy themselves harvesting seeds. Continually pumping its tail, the American pipit walks through meadows, often alone, and visits snowfields to snap up insects immobilized on the cold surface.

The Clark's nutcracker, named for Captain William Clark of the Lewis and Clark expedition, is a loud and flashy member of the crow family. Very fond of whitebark pine nuts, nutcrackers have learned with typical crow ingenuity to utilize many other food sources.

Prairie falcons sometimes hunt over Logan Pass, scanning the meadows for mice and ground squirrels. Larger hawks such as rough-legged and red-tailed hawks are rarely seen here.

Clark's nutcracker.
TOM J. ULRICH

Rosy finch. TOM J. ULRICH

Golden eagles nest in the high country of Glacier, where mountain climbers have literally stumbled over nests and chicks. A spectacular event is the annual golden eagle migration over the park. In October of 1994 more than 2,200 eagles were counted from Mount Brown, a few miles west of Logan Pass. A visitor to Logan Pass in October can enjoy prime views of these high-flying birds.

The male white-tailed ptarmigan is the only bird to spend the winter at Logan Pass; females migrate a short distance to lower slopes during the coldest months. Only a black bill and black eye interrupt the solid white of the ptarmigan's winter plumage. The mottled brown, gray, and white plumage of the ptarmigan in summer matches its surroundings almost perfectly.

Ptarmigan left to right: winter, spring, and summer plumage. MICHAEL S. SAMPLE

Mid June

Hidden Lake ice-out.

What kinds of flowers grow here?

From June to September as many as 200 species of flowers may be found in bloom at Logan Pass. Yellow glacier lilies alternate with white spring beauties in early summer. Red, yellow, and pink blooms of heath arrive later, and patches of sky blue gentians speckle the meadows. Exquisite alpine poppies and Jones columbine grow among the rocks, and it is a rare treat to encounter one.

The amazing variety of flowering plants is explained by the variety of habitats. Wet meadows, scree slopes, damp and cool cliffs, and the banks of perennial streams all create niches for different species. At Logan Pass there are arctic-alpine plants from the north, Pacific Northwest plants from the west, continental plants from the Rocky Mountains, and Great Plains plants from the east.

Alpine plants are well-adapted for surviving and reproducing during the brief summer. Many plants develop flower buds in the fall of the year, so the plant is ready to bloom at the first touch of summer's warmth and moisture. Mountain pasque flowers, for example, often bloom before the snow melts.

Some plants are adapted to live among the rocks, growing close to the ground where the temperature is a few degrees warmer. Alpine plants grow best when above-ground parts get plenty of sunshine and below-ground parts get plenty of water. Most of the water comes from melting snow.

MICHAEL S. SAMPLE

Mid June

Glacier lilies (pictured) begin to appear beneath the snow. Western spring beauty begins to bloom on wind-swept slopes.

Right:
Explorer's gentian.
Michael S. Sample

Above: Elephanthead. Michael S. Sample

Left: Aster, arnica, Lewis' monkeyflower and
Indian paintbrush. Michael S. Sample

Is the water here safe to drink?

Even though the streams at Logan Pass are clear and sparkling and seem to flow directly from the snowfields, the water here is not reliably pure. Visitors should drink only the treated water provided at the visitor center, or bring their own.

The major concern with surface water is the presence of a parasite known as *Giardia lamblia*, causing the disease giardiasis. Anyone who has been struck down by this flu-like ailment will make sure they never drink untreated water again. Portable water filters used by campers may remove giardia, but do not always eliminate bacteria that may cause other serious illnesses. Boiling water and adding iodine are other methods of water purification.

So-called fossil water, flowing directly from glacial ice hundreds of years old, has been described as the world's purest water. Even these sources, however, can be contaminated and should not be drunk without treatment.

Right: Running water over sedimentary layers.
MICHAEL S. SAMPLE

Opposite page: Creek below Reynolds Mountain.
MICHAEL S. SAMPLE

Mid June

Peak runoff at Weeping Wall.

What other
animals
may be seen?

Rocky Mountain bighorn sheep, once rare at Logan Pass, are now seen frequently. Sheep favor dry habitats and exhibit a special preference for the moraines near Clements Mountain. They may have moved into the area because of their expanding population; warmer and drier weather may also have influenced their wanderings.

Mule deer are occasional visitors here. With the sheep, they live in the high country in the summer and move to lower elevations in winter. "Mulies," as they are often called, have big ears; when alarmed, they bound away in great leaps, as if mounted on springs. This unusual gait is known as "stotting."

Pikas, also called "rock rabbits," "little chief hares," and "conies," live in rock slides. They spend the summer cutting and expertly drying vegetation for use in the winter, when they live beneath the rocks and snow. An average pika, weighing about four ounces, stores about 30 pounds of vegetation for winter use.

The wolverine, a large and bad-tempered member of the weasel family, resembles a small bear. Though a wolverine sighting is always special, these animals are seen by visitors every year at the pass, especially near Hidden Lake.

Bighorn sheep. MICHAEL S. SAMPLE

Above: Mule deer at sunset.
MICHAEL S. SAMPLE

Left: Pika.
DONALD M. JONES

Late June

Female ptarmigans seen with brood of chicks.

Late June

Ptarmigans lose white plumage of winter, replacing it with mottled brown, black, and tan summer plumage.

Is Logan Pass
different compared to
other places
in Glacier National Park?

Logan Pass is definitely different from any other place seen by 99 percent of park visitors. The vast expanse of open meadow at high elevation, the gently sloping terrain, and the accumulation of soil permitting the lush growth of low plants is duplicated very rarely in Glacier National Park. Most of Glacier's mountain country is steep, with abrupt slopes and narrow valleys; flat areas, necessary for development of tundra-like vegetation, are rare. The Logan Pass area is a perennial wet meadow, while other alpine meadows in Glacier tend to dry out in late summer and fall.

Red Eagle Pass, south along the divide, has some similarities to Logan Pass, though the meadows are much smaller and the pass is inaccessible to all but the most dedicated hiker. Fifty Mountain, north along the divide and covered with glacier lilies, is not so well-watered and supports different vegetation. East Flattop, the long, flat mountain north of St. Mary Lake, is higher than Logan Pass, but it, too, is much different. There the dryness typical of the east side of the park has caused the development of a prairie–alpine environment.

Right: Lupine, Indian paintbrush and arnica. MICHAEL S. SAMPLE

Opposite page: Subalpine meadow with glacier lilies, Logan Pass. ED COOPER

Early July

Wildflowers in Two Dog Flats area nearing peak blooms. Look for sweetvetch, lupine, arrow-leaf balsamroot, sticky geranium, and blanketflower, among many others.

Was there a
trail over Logan Pass
before the road?

An old trail can be seen north of the road at Logan Pass, extending three miles east to Siyeh Bend. Before construction of Going-to-the-Sun Road, hikers and horseback riders used this trail to visit backcountry chalets and tent camps. A route leading from Going-to-the-Sun Chalets (modern Sun Point) divided east of Logan Pass: one branch crossed Piegan Pass en route to Many Glacier, while the other, the trail seen above the road, crossed Logan Pass and continued on to Granite Park. This trail was constructed in 1918 and abandoned when the road opened in 1933. The continued presence of this very old trail demonstrates the amount of time required for native vegetation to reclaim a disturbed area.

From the west side, another old trail followed Logan Creek, crossing the present road at Oberlin Bend. Apparently this was a trail for trappers and hunters before the establishment of the park; it has not been maintained or used for many decades.

Before the days of modern radio communication, a telephone line reached Logan Pass from the east. The line was then buried to Hidden Lake and continued cross-country to Avalanche Creek, where it joined the main line along the road. Traces of the old line can still be seen toward Hidden Lake.

Right: Looking east toward Logan Pass. MICHAEL S. SAMPLE

MICHAEL S. SAMPLE

Mid July

Highline Trail (pictured) usually opens first weekend after Fourth of July holiday.

Is the **weather** *the same* *east* and *west* of the Continental Divide?

The old saying, "mountains make their own weather," is true at Logan Pass. Straddling the Continental Divide, the pass is influenced by maritime weather from the west and by arctic weather from the north. These two systems often collide along the divide, causing precipitation and unsettled weather. Snow and freezing temperatures usually occur every month of the year at Logan Pass.

The east side of Glacier is sunnier, windier, and cooler than the western half. A typical weather cycle begins with a mass of Pacific air piling up along the western side of the mountains. This air mass cools as it is lifted by the rise in elevation, with rain or snow falling as a result. Precipitation increases along with elevation, and since Logan Pass is the highest point on the road, more rain and snow can be expected here. As the Pacific air mass

becomes drier with the loss of moisture, the air warms and rushes downslope, becoming the legendary chinook winds, or "snow-eaters" to the Blackfeet. These powerful blasts may reach hurricane force and bring a dramatic change in temperature within a few hours.

Sudden shifts between chinook conditions and arctic cold fronts are a way of life in this region. A temperature swing of 100 degrees in one day happened near Browning, on the Blackfeet Indian Reservation just east of the park. This change, from 44 degrees to 56 degrees below zero on January 23, 1916, remains a national record.

June is the wettest month of the summer at Logan Pass. Most visitors will be happy to learn that July and August are the driest months of the year in the mountains.

Mountains building weather over Logan Pass. ED COOPER

When and why was
the boardwalk built?

The present boardwalk, 3,700 feet long and used annually by many thousands of hikers, was built between 1971 and 1973. Before that, a portion of the trail was paved with asphalt.

Twenty-five years ago trails led everywhere at Logan Pass. No attempt was made to direct the ever-increasing numbers of visitors until park managers realized that up to 400 people per hour were hiking toward Hidden Lake on busy summer days. The number of visitors is now much greater and the boardwalk is a success. Hikers traveling from the visitor center to Hidden Lake Overlook should stay on the boardwalk.

The need for a boardwalk at Logan Pass illustrates a basic conflict facing the National Park Service. When the NPS was established in 1916, it was directed by Congress "to conserve the scenery and the natural and historic objects and the wild life therein and to provide for the enjoyment of the same in such manner and by such means as to leave them unimpaired for the enjoyment of future generations." There is obviously much room for interpretation of this mission statement.

The boardwalk is an attempt to protect the fragile alpine environment and, at the same time, accommodate the many visitors who wish to see that environment. George C. Ruhle, long-time park naturalist, has called the boardwalk a "worthy experiment."

MICHAEL S. SAMPLE

Mid July

Indian paintbrush (pictured), yellow arnica, veronica, sky blue gentians, and heather begin to bloom in the meadows around Logan Pass.

Boardwalk, Logan Pass.
MICHAEL S. SAMPLE

MICHAEL S. SAMPLE

Mid July

Fields of glacier lilies in bloom.
Lewis' monkeyflower (pictured)
in bloom.

What are those
little **animals** like gophers?
And the **fat ones**
on rocks?

The small, furry creatures usually seen sitting up, chirping, and begging near the visitor center are Columbian ground squirrels, not gophers. Also known as "picket pins" or "red noses," they are year-round residents at Logan Pass, though active and visible for only about three months of the year. During this time they are busily feeding on grasses, seeds, and other native vegetation. They disappear in August or September, denning below ground for a long sleep of nine months.

The larger animals are hoary marmots, found only in the mountains and never far from rock slides. Constant eating in preparation for winter makes them extremely fat by summer's end. Marmots are more often heard than seen; their shrill whistles are familiar summertime sounds among the rocks at Logan Pass.

Another hibernator is the golden-mantled ground squirrel, often described as a plump chipmunk. While they are in fact related, a golden-mantled ground squirrel has no stripes on its face. All squirrels and chipmunks readily adjust to the presence of humans.

Ground squirrels and marmots are dependent upon natural vegetation to prepare themselves for long hibernation. Feeding all wildlife is not only illegal but harmful to the animals; violators are subject to a fine and a ticket.

MICHAEL S. SAMPLE

Mid July

Beargrass begins to flower in high country.

Above left: Hoary marmot.
MICHAEL S. SAMPLE

Above right: Golden-mantled
ground squirrel.
DONALD M. JONES

Right: Columbian ground squirrel.
MICHAEL S. SAMPLE

Why is the Canadian flag flying at Logan Pass?

Glacier's northern boundary, about 40 miles from east to west, is the 49th parallel of north latitude—the United States-Canada international boundary. Glacier National Park in Montana and Waterton Lakes National Park in Alberta together form Waterton-Glacier International Peace Park, conceived in 1932 to commemorate peaceful relations between the two countries.

Glacier and Waterton are cooperating partners as well as good neighbors. Recently the peace park was included in the international program of Biosphere Reserves. These reserves safeguard parts of ecosystems where conservation of genetic diversity and scientific research are encouraged.

Montanans and Albertans usually account for 30 to 40 percent of all visitation to Glacier National Park, far exceeding the numbers from any other state or province. The exchange rate of the Canadian dollar for the U.S. dollar has a strong effect on Canadian visitation. In 1994, when the Canadian dollar lost value, Albertans accounted for only five to seven percent of total travel. In 1993, with a more favorable exchange rate, Albertans made up seventeen percent of the total.

Opposite page:
Wildflowers along
Logan Creek.
Michael S. Sample

Michael S. Sample

What is
the story of
beargrass?

Beargrass is well named scientifically, but its common name is misleading. The scientific name, *Xerophylum tenax*, means "dry leaves that cling," an accurate description of the plant's rough and dry barbed leaves.

Some authorities claim that bears feed on young plants, though there are no reliable observations of such activity. Even if they did, beargrass is a lily and not a grass. Nevertheless, beargrass as a name is here to stay and it is the unofficial park flower of Glacier National Park. A better name is Indian basketgrass, since American Indians wove watertight baskets from the leaves.

Nowhere is beargrass so spectacular as in Glacier. In some

years, flowering beargrass covers the rocky slopes north of the road at Logan Pass. Scattered plants bloom in the Hanging Gardens. When the open slopes above Going-to-the-Sun Road burst into bloom, the five-foot-tall, fragrant, creamy white flowers are an unforgettable sight.

Summers with heavy beargrass blooms are outnumbered by years of less-dramatic shows. Weather is probably a major factor, but the erratic appearance of flowering stems is not easy to explain. After a stem flowers, it dies, and other stems on the same plant may not appear or flower for several years.

Beargrass in full bloom above Hidden Lake. MICHAEL S. SAMPLE

Why are the rocks
different **colors?**
What causes the **wavy** *formations?*

All of the rocks seen from Logan Pass are Precambrian in age. Known as the Belt Series or Supergroup, these are among the best-preserved ancient sedimentary rocks on earth.

The Helena Formation, ranging in color from gray to tan to brown, may be seen from the boardwalk en route to Hidden Lake Overlook. The varying colors of the Helena Formation indicate the depth of water when sediments were deposited: dark-colored rock means deeper water or flooding, while light-colored rock means drought or shallow water.

Above the Helena rocks, the green and red argillites of the Snowslip Formation extend upward on Clements and Reynolds Mountains. The green and red hues are caused by iron in different chemical combinations. Again, the depth of water during deposition controls the color of the rocks. Little or no oxidation happens in deep water and the result is the green of oxygen-poor compounds; the red shade is caused by the oxidation (rusting) that occurs when iron is deposited in shallow water.

Along the trail to Hidden Lake, mud cracks, ripple marks, and rain spatters are faithfully preserved from the time of their formation in the sea more than a billion years ago. The same process can be seen along the edges of seasonally dry ponds in late summer and fall.

Rock patterns that resemble Brussels sprouts or geometrical swirls are the remains of algae, some of the first plants on earth. These strange designs are more like imprints than actual fossils, since none of the original plant material is left. What remain, though, are true reproductions of these ancient organisms.

Left: Mud cracks. MICHAEL S. SAMPLE

Right: Ripples in rock below Clements Mountain.
MICHAEL S. SAMPLE

Are the glaciers shrinking?

The glaciers in Glacier National Park are much smaller than they once were. In the middle of the nineteenth century, when area glaciers were larger than at any other time in the past 10,000 years, about 150 glaciers were present. Less than half that number remain today, and the total may be as low as 50.

At Logan Pass, Clements Glacier was the last to disappear; its remnants still cling to the base of Clements Mountain. Stationary and comprising more snow than ice, these remains are now classified as parts of a perennial snowfield.

A steady retreat of the park's glaciers began by 1860, accelerated rapidly from the 1920s through the 1940s, and continues today. Some of the larger glaciers increased their size slightly during the 1960s and 1970s, but in recent years the trend has again been one of retreat. The demise of the glaciers is a direct result of above-average summer temperatures and below-average precipitation in the region.

Crevasse in Sperry Glacier. Michael S. Sample

Michael Javorka

August

Huckleberries in Glacier begin to ripen.

Mid August

Cow parsnip in bloom; grizzly bears dig up and eat the roots of this plant.

Why do the
mountain goats
seem so
tame?

All of the wildlife at Logan Pass is wild, not tame. The mountain goats seem to be tame since they apparently do not fear people. They have become *habituated* to humans—a major problem for the park.

A mountain goat habituated to people will lose some of its ability to locate natural food, and may develop an appetite for human food or other manmade substances. Habituated mountain goats consume sweet-tasting antifreeze on park roads. Dogs and cats often die after lapping up this substance, which contains toxic ethylene glycol. The effect of antifreeze on mountain goats is unknown at this time, though it can only be harmful in the long term.

Mountain goats are also drawn to salt. Natural salt licks occur in Glacier and are well known to many animal species, but goats seem to have a special ability to find other sources. Human urine along trails and roadsides forms salt concentrations. If enough urine collects in one area, an unnatural salt lick is formed and mountain goats will associate people with the salt they crave, further increasing their level of habituation. At Logan Pass, all visitors should use the toilet facilities at the visitor center and Hidden Lake.

Habituated animals create problems in many places around the park. Rangers have been forced to kill deer, bears, mountain lions, and other animals when their close association with visitors has made them dangerous. Habituation of all wild animals everywhere is undesirable, and park visitors should do all they can to reduce this hazard.

Mid August

Last of Big Drift usually melts away.

Above: Mountain goat.
MICHAEL S. SAMPLE

Left: Mountain goats in Glacier's high country.
DONALD M. JONES

Is it possible to see a
glacier from
Logan Pass?

Until the 1940s visitors hiking toward Hidden Lake crossed the lobe of Clements Glacier, about three-fourths of a mile from the visitor center. This glacier has since melted back to the base of Clements Mountain.

In most years, the remnants of Clements Glacier fill the basin out to the moraine until midsummer. Melting then reduces the snow to patches of gray seen in September. Some of this perennial snow may be hundreds of years old and covered with rocks, insects, and ancient windborne debris. New snow, or snow of the previous winter, is much whiter.

Standing at Logan Pass and looking slightly west of north along the Continental Divide, Gem Glacier can be seen through a break in the Garden Wall. Only a few acres in size, Gem is tucked into a high pocket just above the much-larger Grinnell Glacier in the Swiftcurrent Valley.

The best roadside view of a glacier is from Jackson Glacier Viewpoint, 4.5 miles east of Logan Pass. Jackson and its neighbor, Blackfoot Glacier, once were joined. Separated today, they still rank among the largest glaciers in the park.

Sperry Glacier, another of the larger glaciers, is visible from Hidden Lake Overlook and from the road near Avalanche Creek. Due to recent melting, Sperry, too, is in retreat.

Hanging Garden in fall colors. JOHN REDDY

September

Fall colors begin to appear on aspen, mountain ash, maple, birch, and cottonwood trees.

Is Glacier always this **busy** and **crowded**?

More than 2,000,000 people visit Glacier National Park every year, and almost all of them stop at Logan Pass. Sunday is the busiest day of the week; the first week of July is the busiest week of the year; and July is the busiest month of the year. Rangers at the visitor center talk to about 3,000 people on an average day and many other visitors are not contacted. These facts and figures mean that on a warm, sunny day in early July, 20,000 people may stop at Logan Pass.

When Going-to-the-Sun Road opened in 1933, a total of 76,000 people toured Glacier. Today, with about 30 times as many visitors, the road is essentially unchanged—a narrow, winding, two-lane thoroughfare. Meanwhile, recreational vehicles seem to grow longer, higher, and wider each year. Visitor numbers rise almost every year. Glacier's historic road cannot handle today's large ve-

Hidden Lake Overlook.

Tour bus on Going-to-the-Sun Road.
GLENN VAN NIMWEGEN

hicles without a major redesign, which would damage the natural and cultural values of the area.

Park officials have moved to address some of these problems. New vehicle size restrictions are in effect on Going-to-the-Sun Road. Vehicles longer than 21 feet and wider than 8 feet are prohibited on the road between Avalanche Campground and the Sun Point parking area. In August of 1995, the parking area at the Logan Pass Visitor Center will undergo renovation and expansion. Much of the park's infrastructure shows its age, and additional road repairs will take place over the next several years.

Mid September

Grizzly bears may often be viewed (through a spotting scope) from Logan Pass Visitor Center.

Where do people hike *from* here?

Most Logan Pass visitors walk to the Hidden Lake Overlook and back—a three-mile excursion—and call it a day. In the mountains, elevation gain means at least as much as distance, and the hike to the overlook climbs to 7,140 feet, 500 feet higher than Logan Pass. This can be a steep grade for some people. Nevertheless, a hike to the overlook and back is a wonderful introduction to Glacier's high country, and anyone with the slightest inclination to walk should spend a few hours and make the trip. For many people it is the highlight of their visit to Glacier.

A more difficult hike begins at the overlook and descends to Hidden Lake, 800 feet below. Hikers following this trail will do most of their work on the return trip.

Some hikers cross the road and hike out along the Highline Trail. Paralleling the Continental Divide and clinging to the Garden Wall, the Highline is one of Glacier's most popular trails. Granite Park, where the chalet is closed for renovation, is eight miles down the Highline. Just beyond is Swiftcurrent Lookout, the square structure atop the conical mountain visible from Logan Pass.

Trails from Granite Park lead over Swiftcurrent Pass to Many Glacier and south to the Loop on the Going-to-the-Sun Road. The Highline Trail ends at Fifty Mountain, 20 miles away, where it splits into the Flattop Trail and the trail to Waterton Lake. Most of these trips are overnighters, though some hardy hikers have walked the 30 miles from Logan Pass to Waterton Lake in one long day.

September

Migrating golden eagles (pictured) begin to pass through Glacier.

Tom J. Ulrich

Above: Hidden Lake.
DARRIN SCHREDER

*Left: Clements Mountain
and backpackers.*
DARRIN SCHREDER

September 30

Logan Pass Visitor Center
closes for the year.

Do grizzly **bears** live here?

Glacier is home to the grizzly bear, and the presence of this remarkable and increasingly rare animal makes the park a special place. Grizzlies are seen in late spring and throughout summer and early fall in the Logan Pass vicinity. During late summer and fall they are busy adding a thick layer of fat in preparation for six months of hibernation. Most grizzlies in Glacier dig their dens at or near treeline, excavating horizontally on slopes of about 30 degrees. Deep snow adds insulation; the temperature in a den will probably remain above freezing throughout the winter.

Some park grizzlies are year-round residents of the high country, with time out in the spring for feeding forays at low elevations. Other bears live year-round at low elevations and never visit the mountains.

Mature Glacier grizzlies weigh about 500 pounds. A notable exception was the famous "Geifer Grizzly," a marauder back in the 1970s that weighed approximately 900 pounds when shot in British Columbia. Bear populations reached their lowest point about the time the park was established in 1910, and their numbers have slowly increased since then. An estimated 200 grizzlies now live in and near Glacier, though authorities disagree on the exact population figure. Grizzly numbers may again be declining as development on all sides of the park eliminates suitable habitat. The grizzly bear is a federally-listed threatened species in the lower 48 states.

Grizzlies are inherently dangerous to people. A sow (female) bear with cubs is very protective, as are bears feeding on a carcass. Much of the trouble between grizzlies and humans occurs when bears become conditioned to accept unnatural food, or when people surprise bears along a trail or in camp. Every precaution possible must be taken to avoid exposing bears to garbage, handouts, or other human-generated food sources.

Hikers in Glacier should make plenty of noise along the trail to avoid a surprise encounter. What do you do if you meet a grizzly? Only sugges-

Sow and cub tracks.
Michael S. Sample

Adult grizzly bear.
DONALD M. JONES

tions can be made, since every situation is different and bears are highly unpredictable. A bear is agitated when it stands its ground and clacks its teeth. A bear with aggressive intent will lower its head. Never stare at a bear and do not run—back away slowly. If the bear charges, drop to the ground in a fetal position with hands locked around the back of your neck. Do not move until the bear leaves.

Pepper spray is used by more and more backcountry travelers in Glacier. It has been effective in some cases and does not permanently harm bears. However, pepper spray is not a substitute for safety precautions and never removes all chances for an encounter.

Early October

Golden eagle migration peaks; as many as 300 eagles per day may pass through the park when flight conditions are favorable.

What do grizzly bears eat?

Andy Russell, who observed, hunted, and photographed grizzlies for many years, wrote, "the grizzly joins man, the hog, and the common rat in being the four outstanding omnivores on earth." In other words, a grizzly bear will eat most anything.

In early spring the high country is covered with snow and food is scarce. Exceptions are the occasional mountain goat, bighorn sheep, mule deer, or elk killed in an avalanche and dug up and devoured by hungry bears. As vegetation turns green, some grizzlies feed on new growth in low meadows, moving higher as the snow melts. Cow parsnip is an important early-season food; grizzlies eat both the stems and roots of emerging plants.

At Logan Pass, bears feed on grasses, sedges, and leafy plants in June. Later they harvest roots, bulbs, and berries. Glacier lily roots are a preferred food for grizzlies, though bitter-tasting to people. Spring beauty bulbs, tasty to humans and bears alike, are also favorites, though less abundant than glacier lilies. The roots of yellow hedysarum are very important grizzly food. Hedysarum grows at all elevations in the park and is very common at some higher, arid locations.

Grizzlies savor all berries, even those decidedly unpleasant to human tastebuds. People ignore buffalo berries due to their bitter, soapy flavor, but grizzlies relish them. Buckthorn berries, even more bitter to us, are another favorite. Bears consume great quantities of huckleberries, a variety also popular with humans. During years of abundant yields, grizzlies compete with people for the harvest. Mountain ash berries, bear berries, raspberries, even currants and gooseberries—all will be gobbled up by grizzlies as soon as they ripen.

Grizzlies are hunters as well as scavengers. Old and weak animals are occasional victims of grizzly attack and young deer or elk may

Grizzlies dig up the bulbs and roots of cow parsnip and other plants.
MICHAEL S. SAMPLE

Grizzly sow and cub. Donald M. Jones

become prey as well. The scent of dead and decomposing animals quickly draws grizzlies. A carcass guarded by a grizzly bear is always a potentially dangerous situation for people.

Although territorial, some grizzlies forget their boundaries at certain times and gather in the high country, attracted to concentrations of nutritious army cutworm moth larvae. The moths migrate from the plains to the high peaks, accumulating there in vast numbers beneath talus fragments. Experienced mountaineers know it is possible to meet a grizzly atop even the highest peak.

Late October

Going-to-the-Sun Road closes after the third Sunday of the month.

When does the Going-to-the-Sun
Road open
and close?

The seasonal cycle is not evenly divided at Logan Pass. Winter usually lasts for six months, stretching from November through April. Some winters begin in earnest in October and persist into May.

The earliest date Going-to-the-Sun Road has opened is May 16; the latest closing date is November 16. Weather and the avalanche hazard determine the opening date. The road must be relocated every spring; sentinels posted during the initial road clearing watch for avalanches. Experienced bulldozer operators are guided by tall "snowstakes," placed over the summer, and by recognition of natural landmarks.

The road has closed as early as October 4, but maintenance crews now work keep it open until the third Sunday in October if at all possible. The road will close on this date even if the weather is mild, since maintenance crews need time to remove guardrails and complete other work before the snow becomes too deep.

Heavy snows can come at any time of year. A June storm in 1966 is still remembered for delivering two to three feet of snow, closing the park for days. A light snow or two is not

Storm over Clements Mountain.
MICHAEL S. SAMPLE

Big Drift. Tom J. Ulrich

uncommon in July, but usually only a few inches will fall. Two feet of snow in August of 1992 and three feet on October 2-3, 1994, caused temporary road closures.

Glacier's mountains are big enough to make their own weather. As mountaineer J. Gordon Edwards says, "plan for the worst and hope for the best."

Early November

Hidden Lake freeze-up.

Why are so many
bicycles on the
road?

When engineers designed Going-to-the-Sun Road in the 1920s, they could never have imagined the sizes and shapes of the cars, trucks, and recreational vehicles that would travel the road in years to come. Nor did they anticipate the popularity of Logan Pass as a destination for bicyclists.

Every year bicycle tours bring more and more cyclists to the park. Conflict occurs when large numbers of motor vehicles and bikes are on the road together. Much of this inconvenience is avoided by restrictions on bicycle use from June 15 to Labor Day. During that time, bicycles are not allowed on Going-to-the-Sun Road from 11 AM to 4 PM between Apgar Campground and Sprague Creek Campground, and between Logan Creek and Logan Pass.

Despite these restrictions, some minor traffic delays are bound to happen. When motorists complain, bicycle enthusiasts are quick to point out that they are non-polluters, using only muscle power as they tour the park. Motorists must acknowledge the dedication and

Mid November

Some grizzly bears enter dens for winter hibernation.

MICHAEL S. SAMPLE

Cyclists pass the Weeping Wall on Going-to-the-Sun Road.
GLENN VAN NIMWEGEN

endurance that go into pedaling from Lake McDonald to Logan Pass—a ride encompassing 3,400 feet of elevation gain.

Bicyclists must observe all traffic laws and comply with park regulations designed to reduce traffic congestion.

Late January

Grizzly bear cubs are born in winter dens.